Everywhere Present and Filling All Things

Come explore the beauty of God's creation as you color images of nature

-Agape Book Cafe-

Everywhere Present and Filling All Things
ISBN 978-1-970709-01-8

This book belongs to:

_____

Can anyone hide
himself in secret
places,
So I shall not see him?"
says the Lord;
"Do I not fill heaven
and earth?" says the
Lord.

Jeremiah 23:24

God is everywhere present and
filling all things. He is...

...in the sun

...in the flowers

...in the trees

...in the big animals

...in the small animals

...in the insects

...in the birds

...in the fish

...in the reptiles

...in the rainbows

...in the ocean

...in the desert

...in the mountains

...in the moon and stars

God is present

...in YOU!

Draw a picture of yourself!

www.ingramcontent.com/pod-product-compliance
Lightning Source LLC
Chambersburg PA
CBHW041129120626
46547CB00019B/2923